Esther Troeder

A Biographical Sketch

David Lear

Esther Troeder: A Biographical Sketch

David Lear

2022 Edition

ISBN-13: 9798404491531

Contents

Acknowledgements

Introduction

Thousands – perhaps millions – of people have seen Esther without realising. In July 1941 she attended the wedding between Miep Santrouschitz, her office colleague, and Jan Gies. Upon leaving the wedding, two photos were taken of Esther as she walked alongside a young girl. The girl was Anne Frank, and the two photos that showed her along Esther have been reproduced across the internet, in magazines, and in countless books, including editions of Anne Frank's famous diary.

I first came across Esther through the Facebook group *Anne Frank Remembered*. On their pages were a handful of photos of Esther, who worked for Anne Frank's father, Otto. Esther often appeared in photos alongside some of those who would hide with Anne Frank, such as Hermann van Pels, and she appeared alongside the likes of Bep Voskuijl and Miep Gies who, just a year or so later would risk their lives to help those in hiding.

Yet, for all this, almost nothing was known of Esther – where she was born, how old she was, and even her surname, were all unknown. At least one member of the *Anne Frank Remembered* group contacted Anne Frank House, but even they knew almost nothing of Esther – they did not even know her surname.

One important thing that was known was that Esther was Jewish and, like Anne, she was killed by the Nazis. I wanted to piece together Esther's life – one that was cut so brutally short – and I scoured the internet for information. I researched every Esther who (I guessed from photos) was aged between sixteen and twenty-five in 1941, who lived in Amsterdam, and who was killed by the Nazis. I then gathered what information I could, and checked photographs where possible. After months of research, I eventually found a young woman called Esther Troeder. She is, I believe, the young woman who worked for Otto Frank and who was acquainted with Anne.

Over time I began to piece together the life of Esther, this near-forgotten girl seen, quite possibly, by millions. The result of this research is this very slim biography.

I hope you will forgive the lack of information and photos. Unfortunately, there is little online about Esther. Usually, I would not consider publishing a book with so little information about someone, but I feel that there should be something permanent to remember Esther Troeder, an ordinary young woman who was killed by the Nazis.

Author's Note

Please note that I have taken some liberties when trying to piece together Esther's short life. So little is known that, to give a hopefully clearer picture of her, not least her final days, I have used other people's accounts of Westerbork, Sobibor and the long train journey in between. While these accounts are other people's, much of what has been written would also apply to Esther.

Esther Troeder
A Biographical Sketch

Birth and Family

Esther Troeder was born on Thursday March 29th 1923 in Amsterdam, Holland. Her father was Hijman Troeder (born December 17th 1896) and her mother was Saartje Troeder (nee Voet) (born March 26th 1898).

Esther's parents, Hijman and Saartje married on April 12th 1922. At that time, Hijman's occupation was listed as diamond worker.

Hijman and Saartje lived at Waterlooplien 85 III, while Hijman's mother and father, Juda and Geertje, lived along the same street at Waterlooplien 99 II. In Amsterdam many buildings are split into apartments with "I" indicating 1st floor, "II" indicating 2nd floor and so on. Hijman and Saartje's address indicates they lived on the third floor of Waterlooplein 85.

Saartje's parents, Hartog and Esther Voet, also lived in Amsterdam.

Both Juda and Hartog's occupations were given as "workman" at the time of Hijman and Saartje's wedding.

Above is a document written at the time of Hijman and Saartje's wedding, detailing information on both them and their parents.

Less than a year later, on March 29th 1923, just three days after her twenty-fifth birthday, Saartje gave birth to a daughter. Saartje and Hijman named the girl Esther – presumably named after Saartje's mother.

Esther was to be the first and only child of Hijman and Saartje.

Little is known of Esther's childhood – there are no known photos of her as a girl and little in the way of documentation. It is not even known which schools Esther attended.

In 1930, Esther's maternal grandmother, Esther Voet, died. She was around sixty-four years old.

One piece of information that was recorded was a short piece in a local newspaper, celebrating Esther's 12th birthday (see overleaf for a copy of the newspaper cutting). It may be that this particular birthday was celebrated for religious reason. Within Judaism a girl becomes an adult on her twelfth birthday. This sometimes celebrated with a Bat Mitzvah, which is a coming-of-age ceremony.

Morgen 29 Maart wordt onze Dochter
ESTHER TROEDER
12 jaar.
Haar Moeder en Vader.
Amsterdam, 28 Maart 1935.
Waterlooplein 85.

2315—8

A rough translation of the above paper is:

Tomorrow, on the 29th of March, our daughter ESTHER TROEDER will be 12 years old.

Her Mother and Father.
Amsterdam, 28th March 1935.
Waterlooplein 85.

It is likely that Esther left school at around sixteen years of age, going on to college where she enrolled on a secretarial course.

Ancestry

The meaning of the surname Troeder is unclear. It is a rare surname most commonly found in the Netherlands and Germany.

Esther's parents, grandparents and great-grandparents were all born and raised in Amsterdam. Going further back, all Esther's recorded ancestors were born in the Netherlands, with perhaps one exception, Mina Brommet who was born in Hesse, Germany, albeit to Dutch parents.

Esther's Dutch roots can be traced back at least as far as the 1700s, and probably go back a lot further.

In the 1500s and 1600s, after gaining independence from the Spanish Empire, the Netherlands became a place of religious tolerance. This made it an attractive place for Jews who were being persecuted in many other parts of Europe. It is likely that most of Esther's ancestors moved to the Netherlands, especially Amsterdam, from other parts of Europe in the 1500s and 1600s.

The earliest of Esther's "Troeder" ancestors is recorded as Alexander Troeder – Esther's great-great-great grandfather who was born Amsterdam in 1788.

Esther's Time
at College

After the Nazi invasion of Holland, Dutch Jews were, in January 1941, required to put their personal information on what were known as Jewish Council Cards. A copy of Esther's card can be found in Appendix A.

From this card we can see that Esther gained a qualification as a shorthand typist, also known as a stenographer. This qualification is almost redundant now in this computer age, but back in the 1930s and 1940s it was a very useful qualification to have.

There were two main parts to this qualification:

Firstly, there was learning how to write in shorthand. This meant learning how to write in a very abbreviated form, so that if a manager wished to dictate a letter, for example, a person who had learned write in shorthand would be able to write at great speed. Many young women (and they almost always were young women) who learned this skill would, once in employment, adapt the shorthand to make it easier for themselves.

The second part of the qualification was typing – especially touch-typing – where the typist did not even have to look at the typewriter when typing at speed. A typist's ability was often measured in how many words a minute they could type.

Practically, if an office manager wished to dictate a letter, the stenographer would normally write down his dictation quickly on a notepad and then type up the letter – again quickly if necessary.

A shorthand typist might progress to become a secretary who had more responsibility. A secretary would be expected to answer the phone, keep diaries, file documents, and carry out other office duties dictated by her employer.

If Esther left school at sixteen then it would have been around the summer of 1939. Typically, courses for shorthand typists were a year long, so it's likely that

Esther gained her qualification in mid-1940, just after the Nazis had invaded the Netherlands.

To begin with, the Nazis let life carry on as normal for Dutch people but slowly, over the next couple of years, they tightened their grip on the Dutch population, not least on the Jewish population. Esther – like so many Jewish people – was to be greatly affected.

Work

On June 6th 1940 an advertisement was placed in a Dutch newspaper looking for someone who could write shorthand and type. The company was Pectacon, a wholesaler of herbs, mixed spices and pickling salts. Pectacon had been recently set up by Otto Frank – father of the diarist Anne Frank.

Otto ran Pectacon alongside his other company, Opekta, a company that sold pectin, for jam-making, and spices.

It is likely to have been around this time, in mid-1940, that Esther, aged seventeen, gained her qualification in shorthand typing.

A copy of the very small advert, as well as a rough translation can be found on the following page.

Voor   lichte   kantoorwerkzaam-
heden

MEISJE

gevraagd voor tijdelijk. Steno en
typen. Goed handschrift vereist.
Handelsmij. Pectacon N.V., Singel 400, Amsterdam-C.

The above advert roughly translates as follows:

For light office duties

GIRL

**requested for temporary work.   Shorthand and
typing.   Good handwriting required. Company:
Pectacon N.V., Singel 400, Amsterdam-C.**

It cannot be stated with certainty that this advert led to
Esther working for Otto Frank, but given there were
only four women in the office – two of whom had
worked for Otto Frank for years – it is quite likely that
Esther saw the advert, responded and – most likely

after an interview – was successful in gaining the post. It is likely that Esther worked for both Pectacon and Opekta. For ease of reading I will in the main only refer to Opekta when discussing Otto's companies.

The advert stated that the post was temporary, but Esther would end up working for Otto Frank until the end of 1941. The business was growing and it may be that Otto realised he would need Esther on a permanent basis.

On December 1st 1940, Opekta, a growing company, moved to a bigger building at 263 Prinsengracht, in Amsterdam. There, Esther worked in an office alongside colleagues Pine Wuurman, Bep Voskuijl and Miep Santrouschitz (later Miep Gies). Speaking in 1981, Bep thought that part of the reason for Otto's move to larger premises was because he was already looking for somewhere to hide his family.

There are at least five photographs of Esther's time at Opekta. In every photo, while her colleagues often seem rather serious, Esther is always beaming a smile. Two of the five office photos were taken on the same day (though the exact date is unknown) in May 1941. In one (see page 26) she is outside the building, and is linking her arm with Miep, who in turn has linked her other arm with Bep. In the other (see page 27) Esther is sitting in the office with Hermann van Pels, Pine Wuurman, Miep Gies and Bep Voskuijl. Hermann van Pels, along with his wife, Auguste, and son, Peter, would just one year later go into hiding with the Frank family.

Sadly, later on, many of Opekta's records were destroyed, so little is recorded of Esther's time working for the company. Much of the information we have has been gleaned instead from these photos.

Another pair of photos which are very similar to each other, and likely taken within a minute of each other (see pages 35 and 36) show Victor Kugler, Miep, Bep, Pine and Esther who are either working or posing for the photo. Victor Kugler, like Bep and Miep, would later help the Franks when they went into hiding.

In May 1941, Opekta became Gies and Company – A change that seemed innocent enough, but it was part of something that would soon have drastic consequences for Esther.

Left to right: Esther, Miep and Bep.
May 1941 – outside Opekta's offices at 263
Prinsengracht.

Opekta employees in May 1941.

Left to right (back row): Esther, Hermann van Pels, Miep Gies

Front row: Bep Voskuijl

This photo was likely taken on the same day as the photo on the previous page. Note that Miep, Esther and Bep are all wearing the same clothes in both photos.

Miep and Jan's Wedding

On July 16th 1941, most likely while she was still at Gies and Company as it was now called, Esther, who was now eighteen, attended the wedding of Miep Santrouschitz and Jan Gies.

In two famous photos taken on the day of the wedding, Esther can be seen walking alongside Anne Frank. Her resemblance in these photos to Anne's sister, Margot, is uncanny. Many people (on social media and elsewhere) have wrongly assumed that the young lady next to Anne *is* Margot. In truth, Margot was unwell that day, and unable to attend. Margot's mother, Edith, also had to stay home to look after her.

Guests at the wedding of Jan and Miep Gies.

From Left to right: Laurens Nieuwenburg (Miep's foster father), Anna Nieuwenburg (Miep's foster mother), Otto Frank, Irene (Laurens' and Anna's grand-daughter), Anne Frank, Bep Voskuijl, Esther Troeder.

This photo appears in the British edition, and probably other editions, of Anne Frank's diary.

This is a cropped version of the photo on the previous page. Esther is on the right.

This photo was used on the cover of Bep's biography, titled: Anne Frank: The Untold Story. *Sadly (but understandably) the cover was cropped so that only Anne and Bep were in the picture.*

Although there only seem to be two online photos of Esther at the wedding, Miep said, much later in life, "She was still there on my wedding day. I have a lot of pictures of her." Perhaps some more photos of Esther from that special day will surface in the future. It seems likely that when Miep said Esther was "still there" Miep was stating that Esther was still working for Gies and Company at the time of the wedding. Esther would not be there much longer though.

The reception was held the next day by Otto at Gies and Company's Prinsengracht offices. Esther also attended the reception.

Miep and Jan's wedding – July 16ᵗʰ 1941.

Left to right:
Anne Frank, Bep Voskuijl (obscured), Esther Troeder,
Pine Wuurman.

Behind Pine, somewhat obscured, is Auguste van
Pels, who would go into hiding with the Frank family
just a year later.

A close up of the photo on the previous page. This is perhaps the clearest photo of Esther taken during her time working for Otto.

Esther's Dismissal from Gies and Company

Esther's time at Opekta / Gies and Company seems to have been a happy one, and she smiles in every photo that she appears in. Sadly, Esther's time working for Otto's firm was not long. The Nazis had invaded the Netherlands in May 1940 and were soon issuing decrees about who could and could not own businesses or work for them.

Otto had, in May 1940, in an attempt to save the business, put it under the name of his gentile colleagues and made it seem as though Opteka was run by non-Jewish people, such as Jan Gies and Victor Kugler.

Opekta office photo.

From left to right: Victor Kugler, Esther Troeder, Bep Voskuijl, Pine Wuurman, Miep Santrouschitz (later Miep Gies).

This photograph was featured in Miep Gies's autobiography: Anne Frank Remembered. *Sadly, Esther is not mentioned in the book. The photo was taken around the same time as the picture on the previous page.*

Despite not looking towards the camera, Esther is still smiling more than anyone else in the photo.

Unfortunately – due to a Nazi decree that Jewish people could not work for gentiles – Esther, being Jewish, had to leave her post.

Pine Wuurman also left the company before the Franks went into hiding, but Miep's account indicates that Pine was not Jewish, so presumably went of her own accord.

Otto had to leave his post in December 1941, presumably because he was Jewish, and so it may be that Esther had to leave around that time for the same reason.

It must have been pretty devastating for Esther, losing her job, her income, her newfound friends, and being treated like a second-class citizen.

As the Nazi laws on Jewish workers became even harsher, Esther then struggled to find work, and even when she did find something, she was repeatedly made redundant, almost certainly because she was Jewish.

In an interview many years later Miep said: "I remember Esther said goodbye to us. She had to leave because she was Jewish…"

Miep also said of Esther, possibly in another interview: "She said goodbye and we wished her the best. She gave me a box with a mirror, comb and brush from her and her family… She stayed in Amsterdam, but could not find work anywhere else. It was all so painful, you see. You heard about her dismissal [from other jobs] but did not talk about it further."

Left to right: Bep, Miep, Esther and Pine.

*The date of the photograph is unknown but would
have been taken either in 1940 or 1941 while Esther
was working for Otto's firm.*

Portrait Photographs

At some point in 1942, some time after she'd left Otto's firm, Esther visited the famous photographic studio Atelier J. Merkelbach. Until 1942 the studio was run by Jacobus Merkelbach, but after his death that year it was taken over by his daughter Antonia Merkelbach, known informally as Mies. Mies would photograph many important people including Queen Wilhelmina.

The three portrait photographs that were taken can be seen over the next three pages.

In a time when photographs were a fairly rare occurrence, Esther's portraits may have been taken to celebrate her forthcoming marriage, discussed in more detail in the next chapter.

These three photographs, taken in 1942, are the last known photographs of Esther. She was nineteen years old.

Marriage

It was not all bad news for Esther. Despite her difficulties relating to work, she became engaged to Meijer Wertheim. He was a leather worker, and like Esther, was Dutch. At the time, Meijer was living with his parents at Eemsstraat 7 II, in South Amsterdam, a couple of miles away from Esther.

It's uncertain when they became engaged but on August 12th 1942 Esther and Meijer were married.

You can see a photo of Meijer on the following page.

A portrait photo of Meijer Wertheim,
Esther's husband.

On Esther's Jewish Council Card in Appendix A, you can see how her address changed many times after leaving her parents' home along Waterlooplein. First Esther lived at Iepenplein 18 I, then Tugelaweg 95 I, then finally at Pretoriusplien 5 I.

In the space of just ten months, between August 1942, and her deportation to Westerbork in June 1943, Esther moved three times.

You can see a photo (taken in 2021) of Esther and Meijer's final home on the following page.

Pretoriusplein 5 I where Esther and Meijer lived their married life. 5 I indicates they lived on the middle of the these three floors.

Deportation of Esther's Parents

On November 28th 1942 there was a razzia, or round-up of Jewish people, in Amsterdam. Among those rounded up, and likely forced into the back of a truck were Esther's parents, Hijman and Saartje. They were most probably taken to a train station and from there transported to Westerbork.

It is likely that Esther had recently moved out of her parents' home, having just married. Had she remained at home, she would most likely have been deported with them.

Hijman and Saartje were not at Westerbork very long. Just a week and a half later, on December 8th 1942 they were sent by train to Auschwitz.

At Auschwitz, new arrivals were chosen either to live –
for the time being at least – or die. Esther's father,
Hijman, was forty-five years old. Esther's mother,
Saartje, was forty-three. Their three-day journey
through the Netherlands, Germany and Poland to
Auschwitz would have taken its toll. Upon their arrival,
despite only being middle-aged, they were both
immediately selected for the gas chambers. Men and
women were separated, and at some point, Saartje
and Hijman saw each other for the last time before
being led separately to their deaths.

Westerbork

Westerbork was originally set up by the Dutch government in 1939, as a transit camp for people, mainly Jews, fleeing persecution in Germany and Austria.

A year later, when Nazi Germany overran the Netherlands, they took over Westerbork and used it as a transit camp for Jewish people, Roma and Sinti, and other "enemies" of Nazi Germany, before sending them on to more infamous camps like Auschwitz, Sobibor and Bergen Belsen.

By Nazi standards, Westerbork was humane – there was a restaurant, hairdresser, school and orchestra. But these were there mainly to give the inmates a false sense of security.

Westerbork also had a hospital – again this was effectively a trick. Many people were sent to the hospital to recover, only to be sent on to death camps straight afterwards. There are many stories of this happening. For instance, one man tried to commit suicide at Westerbork. Surgeons then worked hard to save his life. The man recovered and eventually left the hospital. A week after being discharged, he was sent to Auschwitz where he was gassed upon arrival.

Within Westerbork, and surrounded by barbed wire, were Barracks 65, 66, and 67 – the punishment barracks. These were reserved for Jews who had not followed the Nazi's decrees, such as those who had gone into hiding and later been discovered, or those who had not worn their compulsory yellow star of David.

Unlike other inmates, those in the punishment barracks were not allowed to keep their own clothes, but were forced to wear wooden clogs and blue overalls. You can see one overall from Westerbork's punishment block on page 54. The overalls had a red number and red material across the shoulders which made any potential escapees very visible and easy targets for anyone hunting them down.

Men and women in the punishment block had their hair shaved, and received no soap. They had less food than other prisoners and were forced to work in the most arduous conditions. These "convict" Jews were also the first to be selected for transportation on the next train to the concentration camps of Poland, leaving on the subsequent Tuesday.

An original overall from the punishment barrack.

Esther's Deportation to Westerbork

Esther would have been hit hard by the deportation of her parents. The fact that she would have received no correspondence from them might well have alarmed her.

In March 1943 Esther celebrated her twentieth birthday, but having already seen her parents and other friends and acquaintances deported, it might not have been celebrated with as much cheer as in previous years. It was also to be her last birthday.

On June 20th 1943, there was a roundup of Jews by the Nazis – possibly Dutch Nazis – and Esther and her husband, Meijer, were most likely told to quickly pack some essentials and leave their home, and then forced into the back of a truck.

For reasons mentioned later in this chapter, it may also be that they were in hiding and were discovered prior to June 20th. If so, Esther and Meijer may well have been sent by truck to the local police station first, and from there to a prison on the Weteringschans. Here men and women were separated. A few days later, reunited, Meijer and Esther would have been sent with other Jews by tram, and then train on a five-hour journey to Westerbork.

Coincidentally, at least three of Anne Frank's friends, Sanne Ledermann, Juultje Ketellapper and Hannah Goslar, were also transported to Westerbork on June 20th 1943. The journey to Westerbork would have taken a few hours.

On arriving, Esther queued with other unfortunates. Her luggage was taken away and she was given a camp pass, and a card with a number on it to get food.

The pass showed a red "H" for Häftling or prisoner. This was most likely because she'd committed some sort of "crime" such as being in hiding and been caught.

On Esther's Jewish council card (which you can see in Appendix A) a handwritten note says that at

Westerbork she was put into Barrack 67 – Barracks 65, 66, and 67 were the so-called punishment barracks.

Another coincidence is that a year later Anne Frank and her family were also imprisoned in Barrack 67.

Meijer seems, according to his Jewish Council Card (see Appendix B) to have been put in Barrack 57 – a different barrack to Esther.

The most likely reason for Esther being put in the punishment barracks was that she and her husband had gone into hiding and been caught. Around a quarter of Dutch Jews went into hiding at some point in the war. It can also be seen from Esther's Jewish Council Card that she moved round a lot, indicating that, unsurprisingly, she was enduring a difficult period in her life. Given her parents deportation, she might well have felt it better to go into hiding.

Like the others sent to the punishment or penal barracks, it is likely that Esther had her hair cropped. In the short time that she was there, she would have also received less food than most inmates.

Here she would, on arrival, have been told to take off her clothes and inspected for lice, and for any contagious diseases.

The penal barracks were fenced off from the rest of the camp. Esther's clothes were taken away, and she was given clogs and an overall with a yellow star of David to wear. The overall also had an "S" on, to show that she was a "punishment" case. The overall also had a red strip on the back, near the shoulders. This was so that if such prisoners tried to escape, the red strip acted as a target for the Nazis to shoot at.

Whereas many people were held at Westerbork for many months, not least families of some importance, Esther and Meijer were held at Westerbork for just nine days.

On June 29th 1943, Esther and her husband were reunited, and made their final journey to the death camp, Sobibor.

The above image is a map of Westerbork transit camp. The penal barracks where Esther was held are at the very top, on the right-hand side.

Sobibor

Sobibor, in Poland, was not a concentration camp like Auschwitz, where people were either killed or allowed to live. Hidden away in a forest, Sobibor was instead an extermination camp – built solely for the purpose of killing Jews.

Most of those who were sent from Westerbork to Sobibor were sent not on ordinary trains but in windowless cattle-trucks.

Sobibor was built along the Lublin-Chelm-Wlodawa railway line just west of the Sobibor railway station. A nearby spur connected the railway to the camp and was used to offload prisoners from incoming transports. A dense forest of pine and birch shielded the site from view.

A minefield surrounded the site, and the barbed-wire fencing was camouflaged with branches woven in.

Trees were planted round the perimeter, so as to obscure the view.

Most Jews were gassed upon arrival. Only a few were allowed to live, for a few months at most, and had to help with the running of the camp.

After the people were gassed to death, their bodies were incinerated. Above these incinerators were chimneys where the flames could be seen. The ashes of the dead were then unceremoniously buried.

The camp was only in operation for a year and a half, but in that time at least 167,000 men, women and children were killed at Sobibor – and the figure could be considerably more.

Of the 34,000 Dutch Jews sent to Sobibor, only 18 survived.

Sobibor extermination camp in the summer of 1943, around the time Esther and Meijer were sent there. It was deliberately made to look pleasant and reassuring.

Esther's Deportation to Sobibor

On Tuesday, June 29th 1943 – having spent just nine days at Westerbork – Esther and Meijer were transported by train from Westerbork to Sobibor extermination camp. Esther's Jewish Council Card has this date of transportation written on it (See Appendix A).

At Westerbork, after being told of their departure, Esther and Meijer would have queued to board one of the windowless cattle-trucks that were to take them to their destination. It is likely that Esther didn't even know where she and her husband were headed.

While we now know what went on at Sobibor and Auschwitz, few people back then knew what was really happening at these places. Esther almost certainly did not know that in just a few days she was going to be killed.

As they queued for the train, people who delayed getting onboard, perhaps through ill-health, fatigue, or fear, were pushed, struck or kicked until they boarded.

Carrying her meagre possessions, most likely including a little food and water, Esther boarded with her husband. Once she and her fellow prisoners were crammed in, the doors were shut, and suddenly they found themselves in almost total darkness. The only light, giving her any sense of vision, would have streamed in through a small barred window.

There was no real toilet, only a single barrel in the corner of the wagon, far too small for everyone to relieve themselves. Sometimes these barrels would spill over to the horror of those in the carriage.

In another corner of the wagon, there was a single barrel of water for the sixty or so people in the cattle-truck to share.

As they travelled through the Netherlands, Germany and finally Poland, the train stopped multiple times to let military and other vehicles cross the tracks.

It is likely that for the entire duration of her journey, Esther was kept in darkness, the wagon doors never being opened until they arrived at their final destination.

As they travelled, the little barrel that served as a toilet would have filled to the brim, and the stench would have filled every part of the truck. Esther would have had to put up with this stench for days. If Esther experienced the same as other recorded accounts, she would have listened to people at the end of their tether crying and arguing, and in all this misery, many people, quite possibly including Esther herself – oblivious to what became known as the Holocaust – would have looked forward to arriving at their destination and getting back out into the sunlight, the open space, and fresh air.

When they finally arrived at Sobibor on July 2nd, after three days of gruelling travel, Esther and her husband got out of the dark cattle-trucks, and were probably momentarily blinded by the summer sun. Esther would have been weak and barely able to walk. Of the dozens of others that shared their truck, some may well have already died – such deaths on this long journey to Sobibor were not uncommon.

The camp's true purpose – mass murder – was disguised, a tactic not dissimilar to that used at Westerbork; the station was decorated with pretty flowerbeds, and new arrivals like Esther were given a friendly welcome speech by an SS officer. The officer would apologise for the long journey and poor conditions they must have endured, and he would tell the prisoners that Sobibor was merely a transit camp, and that the first thing they needed to do after travelling in such filth and squalor, was to be disinfected.

The arrivals were also encouraged to send postcards home, telling their loved ones that they had arrived at a pleasant destination. After the ordeal of the journey, and after the speech, it is known that some of the arrivals clapped with happiness, really believing that they were, for the time being at least, going to be alright.

Men were separated from women and their possessions were given to the camp guards for safekeeping. Around this time Esther saw her husband for the last time.

Before being disinfected, Esther and the other women were made to undress. Given lice was a common problem, not just in people's hair but in their clothes too, this undressing may have seemed reasonable. Certainly no one was in the position to argue. Next, naked and at gunpoint, Esther was marched with fellow prisoners along a path. They were told it led to the "showers".

In a hut along the way, Esther and the other women had their hair cut or shaved off. Some women asked those Jewish prisoners who did the cutting, not to cut it too short. Many of the prisoners cried at losing their hair. The prisoners who did the cutting knew of the fate that was to befall the new arrivals but could not say anything because there were always soldiers present.

The prisoners' hair was to be used by the German army for things such as yarn, socks, slippers and filters.

After her hair had been cut off, in a process that took around half a minute, Esther was marched on for another hundred yards or so, and directed into a building. As more and more people were crammed in, it would have become clear something was wrong. The last few people crammed in may well have been brutally forced in by soldiers. The doors were locked and soon the sound of a diesel engine could be heard. Carbon monoxide was then pumped into the room. People began to scream and tried to escape as they breathed in the toxic fumes and realised something terrible was happening to them. Then the screams would subside.

On July 2nd 1943, Esther and Meijer were both gassed to death.

Esther's lifeless body was taken out and carried to a crematorium where, along with many others, she was burned until she was no more than bones and ashes. Esther's remains were then taken into the woods and buried.

Miep Gies, who helped the Frank family when they were in hiding said simply of Esther: "She did not come back. She did not survive the war."

Despite knowing so little of her, so long as there are photos of the happy, smiling Esther, she will not be forgotten.

Post Script – The Fate of Esther's Family

Esther, who had no brothers or sisters, was not only killed along with her husband, parents and three living grandparents but, having researched the fate of her extended family, it seems also that every one – every single one – of her twenty-four aunts, uncles and cousins were also murdered by the Nazis. Of her family of thirty-one, not a single relative survived the holocaust.

Appendices

Appendix A

Esther Troeder's
Jewish Council Card

WERTHEIM-TROEDER, Esther   J.
~~Iepenplein 18 I~~ Amsterdam Wertheim, Meyer 16·6·19
~~Frijckaweg 95 A Eadorius plein 55~~
29.3.23   Amsterdam
Ned.
stenotyp. Waterl.109 18.7.42
JR A 700 steno-Typ.
Gesperrt wegens: functie
vroegere werkkring: steno-typ.en facturiste
Diploma's: 2 jaar MULO
Indruk: flink ijverig
Bijzonderheden: liberaal
Algem.opmerkingen:

Esther's Jewish council card.

Here is a breakdown of what some of the writing on the Esther's card means:

The date 29.3.23 is Esther's date of birth.

You can see how her address changed many times after leaving her parents' home along Waterlooplein. First Esther lived at Iepenplein 18 I, then Tugelaweg 95 I, then finally at Pretoriusplien 5 I.

Stenotyp. means steno typist (or shorthand typist.)

Indruck: flink ijverig means "Impression: quite diligent"

Near the top right corner is 20/6/43 WBK. This is the date that Esther was deported to Westerbork.

Below WBK 20/6/43 is the code Bar 67. Westerbork was split into barracks and Bar 67 means Barrack 67. Barracks 65, 66 and 67 were the so-called penal or punishment barracks where prisoners were treated more harshly than other Westerbork inmates.

The red writing was by the Red Cross, and was written after the war. It is the date that Esther was transferred from Westerbork to Sobibor.

Appendix B

Meijer Wertheim's
Jewish Council Card

Meijer's Jewish council card.

Note that Meijer was put in Barrack 57, a different barrack to Esther.

Acknowledgements

My thanks to Klaas Jan Dijkstra who supplied me with certain pieces of information and helped with translations.

My thanks also to those who have put information on Esther and her family online.   If you have any information on Esther that you might like to share, you can email:

editor@firestonebooks.com

Printed in Great Britain
by Amazon

33620150R00046